# The Viewpoint

# of a Woman

# The Viewpoint of a Woman

## The Window of Your Understanding

Jessie Brown

Printed in the United States of America

ISBN 978-1-935914-03-7

To order additional copies please visit:

*www.riversanctuarypublishing.com*

RIVER SANCTUARY PUBLISHING
P.O. Box 1561
Felton, California 95018

www.riversanctuarypublishing.com
*Dedicated to the spiritual awakening of the New Earth*

# Contents

# *Preface*

## Walk with Me through My Viewpoint

Upon receiving instructions from God along with the title for this book, I began research for the writing and structure of this material – *The Viewpoint of a Woman: The Window of Your Understanding*. I find that many times when God gives us something to do, the material and information is already implanted inside of us. I thank God for inspiring me to embark upon this journey, and trust that the information inside of me will be just and credible; and that the wisdom and knowledge that His word has instilled in me will be acceptable in His sight. The day that He gave me the title for this book, I was surprised, for this was a great task to undertake. But I had confidence in God that whatever He gave me, I would be able to accomplish through Him. Praise God for His word is true. So now, sit back and enjoy the book. I hope and pray that it will enlighten you, and help you to understand that each person's viewpoint is the window of his or her understanding. Remember always that God loves you and will never leave you nor forsake you.

# *Introduction*

## The Window of Your Understanding

One day during the month of March 1999, the Lord spoke to me concerning this book. He gave me a title, *The Viewpoint of a Woman*. Then I began to research and He gave me topics to write about. It took me two years and some months before I began to write the book. As I prepared to write, God spoke to me again and said, "The viewpoint is the window of your understanding." God was not speaking about the natural window pane, but He was speaking about spiritual sight, in which I gained knowledge, discernment and understanding. This is our ability to understand the precepts and parables that are written and spoken about throughout the Bible from Genesis to Revelation. Our ability to conceive is how well we can submit to God the Father. We can find answers to any and all trials or tribulations in our lives. Now let me explain what I have learned. I hope and pray others will benefit from the concepts that God has given to me.

Walk with me as I travel through experiences and events that have occurred on this journey.

This window enhances the complexity of your mind in grasping the knowledge of God's word. In order for our understanding to follow the rules and guidelines of the Father and

Jesus Christ to live a healthy and defined life, we must learn to adhere to the authority of the word. Guidelines are given for instruction in understanding that the One in authority knows the working of the idea better than we do. Therefore, in order to advance to higher ground, we must learn to lay aside worldly opposition and strive to gain knowledge in areas that would benefit us. Only the Holy Bible can instruct us on spiritual things, for when we cannot comprehend the spirituality of the Bible, then we are grasping in darkness. This book contains some knowledge on how to advance in this world from infancy to adulthood in the spiritual realm. We all have to go from stage to stage, or as Paul says "from level to level," for it is a growing process. In order to grow, we must learn to study "to shew ourselves approved, workmen that need not be ashamed, rightly dividing the word of truth." (II Tim. 2:15)

There is a higher power that gives us freedom to make choices for our lives. His standards are not as difficult as man would have us to believe, for He is able to forgive us and lead us out of danger and encamp around us, giving us light to walk this walk, and talk this talk. *The Viewpoint of a Woman* is an idea conceived through the Holy Spirit, giving me the opportunity to share a word of knowledge as I see through this Window of Understanding.

Sometimes it is hard for us to see because of the decisions that we make for ourselves, but we must always remember that God is ultimately in control of everything and everyone. For when He stepped out on the face of the earth and it was void, He, God, decided to create the heavens and the earth, giving it inhabitants to live on and replenish it. Then He created man and woman to multiply his seed upon the earth and take care of the animals He had created. But we know the story of how man and woman fell from the grace of the Lord and were made to toil for their living; when in reality, if they had listened to God, they would not have had to toil and labor for their food and housing.

In the same way today, there are too many bosses and not enough servants. This brings us to the window of your understanding, for it will take us step by step as the Holy Spirit guides me through the word of God. I am sure we know that in order for us to understand the word of God, we have to have already received Christ as the head of our lives. How can we understand the spiritual things of God when we are walking in darkness? I am not talking about day and night, I am speaking in reference to our being unsaved (i.e. not being able to see the light of Jesus Christ). We must be saved. In order to receive this light of understanding, we must adhere to Romans 10:9-10 where it speaks about believing and confessing that Jesus Christ died for our sins. There we are given a chance at eternal life because of it, and confessing that God raised Him from the dead, we are saved. We must repent and confess that Jesus Christ lives and we are saved.

On this walk, we will have trials, tests, longsuffering and hardship, but through it all God's light will lighten our paths, for He said I will never leave you nor forsake you. His word will be a lamp unto our feet and a pathway to life should we learn about Him and govern ourselves accordingly. Romans 8:29-31 says, "For whom he did foreknow he also did predestinate to be conformed to the image of his son, that he might be the firstborn among many brethren. Moreover whom he did predestinate, them he also called: and whom he called, them he also justified: and whom he justified, them he also glorified. What shall we then say to these things? If God be for us, who can be against us?" These instructions compile a lot of knowledge to be gained, for in order to comprehend the wisdom of the word, we must strive to understand the attacks that the flesh is under, for we were born in sin and shapen in iniquity.

Therefore, we know that our enemy, the devil, will attack our minds in order to ensnare us in darkness. Remember the holy word of God will be a defense against his attacks, for He has already given us the greatest weapon of all, His son Jesus Christ, for He has taken and borne all our sins upon Calvary. He died that we may live, and rose from death so that we can live our lives victoriously for God. The attacks of the enemy (Satan) can be dispelled by the promises of God. For Romans 8:31 says, "If God be for us, who can be against us?" Even when the test comes, we must be steadfast, unmovable, always laboring in the vineyard and the word of God for as much as we know our labor is not in vain. Ephesians 6:10-18 says, "Finally my brethren be strong in the Lord, and in the power of his might. Put on the whole armor of God, that ye may be able to stand against the wiles of the devil. For we wrestle not against flesh and blood, but against principalities, against powers, against the rulers of the darkness of this world, against spiritual wickedness in high places. Wherefore take unto you the whole armour of God, that ye may be able to withstand in the evil day, and having done all, to stand. Stand therefore having your loins girt about with truth, and having on the breastplate of righteousness; And your feet shod with the preparation of the gospel of peace; Above all, taking the shield of faith, wherewith ye shall be able to quench all the fiery darts of the wicked. And take the helmet of salvation, and the sword of the Spirit, which is the word of God: Praying always with all prayer and supplication in the Spirit, and watching thereunto with all perseverance and supplication for all saints." Here Paul relates to us how to stand against the wiles of the devil.

Paul understood that we need to know that our weapon is the word of God, for inside the word is peace and comfort. In order for us to gain this peace and stability, we must first learn how to establish a fortress around ourselves by hiding the word of God in our hearts so that, when the devil comes to attack, we can be ready to destroy the power of the enemy. Paul says stand up for what is rightfully yours for God declares that his word shall not return unto him void but will accomplish what he desires to accomplish in our lives, and in it, we will prosper also.

As we continue to look at Ephesians 6:10-18, we find instruction on how to exemplify the authority and power of a holy God. He demands that we understand that control of our lives belongs to Him, but one thing He will not do is force Himself upon us. This relationship is based upon choices and decisions that we make, for it is freedom and liberty that we have received from God through Jesus Christ. Listen to this –God is a spirit, therefore we must serve Him in spirit and in truth. Now that we understand the implications of walking in spirit and truth, we can begin to be sincere in our service to the Lord. We must learn how to stand and exemplify our Lord and Savior. He was an example for us. When He suffered for our sins, He was whipped unmercifully for each of us. God loved us that much, before we were even born.

Man had become so sinful in God's eyesight that He had to plan a way out for His people that would teach us about Jesus and how to accept Him in our lives. We walk by faith and not by sight. Hebrews 11:1 says, "Now faith is the substance of things hoped for and the evidence of things not seen." Therefore, we learn to trust God through His word and the guidance of the living Holy Spirit. Paul says in order to put on this armor, we must first learn that people have different personalities and thoughts, some good and some bad. We must remember it is not the person, but that unruly spirit that dwells in us. When we can surmise that we must dwell with God in spirit, and only through the spirit, then we will be able to stand. Let's look at the word of God so that we can grow up in the spirit and put on the whole armor of God through Christ Jesus, and stay focused through the living Holy Spirit.

I am challenged to expound on these topics to help us gain a viewpoint through the eyes of the Lord in His word. Faith in God through the word will unlock the windows of heaven, through seeking, searching, scripture, submitting, growing, standing and last, but not least, obtaining.

# *Chapter 1*

## Seeking

*But seek ye first the kingdom of God, and his righteousness; and all these things shall be added unto you."*

Matthew 6:33

In our continuous gaining of spiritual heights with God, we must learn to seek His kingdom first. We must seek Him through prayer and supplication, in a humble state of mind.

Let us look at Solomon. When he became king, God was with him, because he sought God's will. Why did God bless Solomon the way he did? Solomon was a praying man, and he knew that in order for him to accomplish what God had proposed and purposed for him to do, he must first seek God's approval. When he did that, God spoke to Solomon and asked him what he desired for God to do for him, and Solomon replied that he would like God to give him wisdom to know how to judge God's people. God told him since he only asked for wisdom, he was going to bless him in all areas of his life. Solomon didn't ask for material things, but spiritual wisdom.

We must know how to answer God when He speaks to us. This brings an incident to mind that happened to me in the past. A close friend of mine gave her daughter a birthday party at

Quiet Waters Recreation Park. We were in a nice clean pavilion and I appreciated that, but in the pavilion below us, there was another group of people celebrating an occasion. One person from that group came and sought my friend's attention about switching pavilions. I tried to tell her not to do it, but she was in control and agreed to switch.

Upon arriving in the other pavilion, we were met with gigantic ants all over the ground and cats coming out of the bushes. I took a hose and began spraying the ants and cats to clear them away so we could have a good time. But my thinking was not pure. I had become annoyed with the other group for pulling such a stunt on my friend, so I said to God, "Lord I hope they don't have a good time," not knowing the consequences would be soon to come.

The sky was clear and the sun was hot and things had begun to settle down until we looked and saw an ominous-looking black cloud heading our way. We began preparing for the worst. Then God spoke to my spirit and said "Pray." I grabbed a couple of sisters' hands, and we began to pray. In the prayer I heard myself say, "Jesus spoke to the winds and waves and said 'peace be still.'" When I said that, the rain and ominous cloud backed off.

Everyone began again to enjoy themselves, and God spoke to me again and said, "Watch what you ask me for, for I will give it to you." From that day to this, when I seek God for any and all things, I ask for his best because I experienced the consequences of wrong seeking, and I shall never do that again.

So my advice to you is never seek God for revenge for He said revenge is His, so saith the Lord. All we need to do is repent for our sins and petition God with a righteous and holy attitude. For your motives are already known to God.

We cannot hide anything from God because He is an all-knowing wise God, and sees us for exactly who we are, so we might as well be clean in seeking God for help.

# Chapter 2

## Searching

*And the brethren immediately sent away Paul and Silas*
*by night unto Berea: who coming thither went into the*
*synagogue of the Jews. These were more noble than those*
*in Thessalonica, in that they received the word with all*
*readiness of mind, and searched the scriptures daily,*
*whether those things were so.*
Acts 17:10-11

I have learned that on this life's journey, the influences that we are exposed to from birth to adulthood can be damaging if we are not equipped with stamina, strength, and good teaching from our parents. Concepts such as responsibility, independence, right decision-making, cooperation and friendship are essential. Something else that should be taught to every child is that education is a very important part of growing up and being a reliable person. It is a concept that adds stability and competence in realizing one's purpose and life plan.

I remember one day as I traveled the path that I had chosen, it became very hard for me to gain the level of understanding that I needed to reach the goals in life that I had set for myself in a given length of time.

So then I began to search inside to find my true self and understand how to change my circumstances. I had been raised up in church and decided when I got grown I would attend church when I got ready. Bad choice, for I have learned that we suffer the consequences of wrong decision-making. It is the choices that we make that will bless us or destroy us. Praise the Lord.

In searching myself, I came to realize that the choice I made in perceiving that I didn't need God in my life was a terrible mistake. I learned that the bad things that happen to me are under the control of the devil, who desires to destroy a person and keep them in a state of confusion. Oh, but in my searching I found a way out. I began to pray and search for spiritual knowledge and understanding for the path that I had chosen. Psalm 139:23 says, "Search me O God, and know my heart: try me, and know my thoughts." This tells me that once I seek the Lord's guidance, he will begin to search and refine me so that I can gain wisdom and knowledge to learn his concepts.

In learning the word, we can accomplish and maintain a greater order in our daily occupation and be able to endure the complexity of life's changes and the choices that we make. The written word of God is a covenant between God and his people. He desires us to search and find Him, so that we can learn about the benefits He has instituted for us to receive and the goodness that He has placed in His word for us to use in gaining wisdom, understanding, and knowledge so that we can live a more peaceful and fulfilling life.

This search involves studying the concepts of the holy word, so that we may improve our level of understanding and overturn the darker areas of our lives into lighter avenues. There is only one avenue that God really wants us to understand and grasp. By learning about his son Jesus Christ and receiving Him in our lives, peace, joy, love, wisdom, understanding, and protection are just a few of the benefits.

How do you know when it is time to begin your search? When you can't gain peace and everything begins to go wrong, and you can't find a way out. Remember Jesus is there to help us and deliver us into a better place, where we will gain instant peace. We also know that the wages of sin are death and the gift of God is eternal life. In other words, He is extending an invitation unto us, telling us that in order to gain heavenly assurance we must receive Jesus Christ in our hearts. For Romans 10:9-10 says, "that if thou shalt confess with thy mouth the Lord Jesus, and shalt believe in thine heart that God hath raised him from the dead, thou shalt be saved. For with the heart man believeth unto righteousness; and with the mouth confession is made unto salvation."

It is hard to live this life without Jesus Christ in our lives, for the spirit of God lives in every person, saved and unsaved. The saved utilize the benefits of God and confess Jesus Christ, and the unsaved continue to rely on themselves.

My hope is that by the time you complete the reading of this book, you will have a better understanding of your viewpoint in the order of life's choices.

# Chapter 3

## Scripture

*Study to shew thyself approved, a workman that needeth not be ashamed, rightly dividing the word of truth.*

II Timothy 2:15

It is imperative that we show ourselves approved. I can remember one day as I studied the word, God led me to Isaiah 50:4 where it is written: "The Lord God hath given me the tongue of the learned, that I should know how to speak a word in season to him that is weary: he wakeneth morning by morning, he wakeneth mine ear to hear as the learned." I have learned also that in order for us to understand what God wants from us, we must learn to hide His word in our hearts that we do not sin against Him. (Psalm 119) I have experienced deliverance through the word of God many times. When reading the scriptures, I allow the Holy Spirit to guide me, for the Holy Spirit knows the working of God's mind. God is a spirit, and we must worship him in spirit and in truth.

The written scripture gives revelation to many events that occur in our lives, for the scripture tells us in I Corinthians 10:13, "There hath no temptation taken you but such as is common to man: but God is faithful, who will not suffer you to be tempted above that ye are able; but will with the temptation also make a way to escape, that ye may be able to bear it."

God says everything that happens to us in this present day has already occurred in another time and place. When we allow Him to lead us through the vineyard of trials and temptations, we are able to withstand anything the devil can throw at us.

When we study and learn the word of God, then we can gain strength and power to hold on throughout the everyday hassles that befall us in our daily occurrences.

In Matthew 22:29, "Jesus answered and said unto them, Ye do err, not knowing the scriptures, nor the power of God." Jesus is telling the people of Israel that they are making errors in judgment about everyday matters. Instead, they need to follow the written scriptures so that they could gain power as well as understanding of problems that arise in life.

I am so glad that reading has never been a problem for me, because now it is an advantage in studying the written scriptures of God. These are binding laws for us because I am convinced that God will honor His word. He has a master plan for this great universe, therefore He has a master plan for our lives. We must be determined to hide His word in our hearts, so that we do not sin against Him in any spoken word or work. And yet we also know that repentance is scriptural, in that we have forgiveness for thoughts and things we should not have done. Denying self is also a necessary part of following God's plan.

In studying the scriptures we learn how to love, be affectionate, kind, compassionate, care about others, gain wisdom, knowledge, understanding, etc. There is so much that reading the scriptures can teach us, for the Bible is "Basic Instruction for the Believer before Leaving Earth."

My advice is that we learn to study every day and gain power in our daily walk with the Lord. For when we don't have the word on the inside to lead us, our choices can be wrong; and in certain instances, our choices may simply be inappropriate. God's word helps us to grow and to stand. We must come up from "the baby and milk stage" into the adult stage of "steak, potatoes and bread" and into the land of milk and honey. Study, study, study!!!

SCRIPTURE: Since Christ Rose In Perfect Triumph Unto Releasing Everyone (from sin).

*Chapter 4*

## Submitting

*Submit yourselves therefore to God. Resist the devil,*
*and he will flee from you.*

James 4:7

Submitting is a very hard subject to digest because you have been in control of your life for a long time, and to think that you have to give control to someone else is not an easy thing to do. Throughout the Bible you will read many parables about circumstances that occur in the lives of different people. In this contemporary world, we are experiencing the same or similar circumstances.

If it was hard for God's people to submit unto Him then, so it is the same today. For God said there hath no temptation overtaken us but such as is common to man; but God is faithful, who will not suffer us to be tempted above that we are able, but will with the temptation also make a way to escape, that we may be able to bear it. (I Corinthians 10:13) God is so merciful unto us that even when we make a wrong choice, He is willing to give us relief from the pressure. We have lived so long making choices that we think are suitable for our well-being, that to allow the Creator to direct us in our walk does not always appear to be a desirable option.

Therefore, it is imperative that we learn how to submit to our Lord and Savior by adhering to the word of God. There we will find many who have learned to submit to the will of God. The Lord broke my will, and I have been submitting ever since. One day, a few years ago, I needed something from God. (At times he will use another person to take care of what you have asked him for.) On this particular day, I was riding with a very special and close friend. We were talking and laughing. I think we were going out to eat, I am not sure. Then God moved upon me through the spirit of the Lord and told me to tell her what I had asked him for. Yet I refused to ask. God, through the Holy Spirit, lifted my hands in the air, and I began to praise God. He spoke to me again and said "Tell her now." I submitted and told her what I had asked God for, and she spoke to me and told me that God had already spoken to her beforehand and she was very happy to oblige. When she said that, I began to praise God for His awesomeness. To love me so much that He would take the time to prove Himself to me, inspired me tremendously. I have submitted gladly from that time forward.

I submit unto you that it is in your best interest to learn how to submit to God through the Holy Spirit in all things in your daily life, for He is the one that created you and gave you the purpose to serve him through Jesus, His only begotten son.

When we don't submit in our walk with God, we will experience the consequences of choices we make which exclude the

Lord. God has ordained many outstanding blessings in our lives. When we submit, we can receive those blessings, and we gain understanding that it is not about us. The will of God in our lives will guide us. The power of God's word in us gives the success that we need to help us become better people in our walk, talk and work for the Lord. Submit and be blessed. Read on and be blessed. Praise God.

*Chapter 5*

## Growing

*As newborn babes, desire the sincere milk of the word,*
*that ye may grow thereby.*

I Peter 2:2

Peter is instructing the children of Israel to study the word of God so that they can deny self and relieve themselves of the wickedness of this world. He knew in order for a person to live well, they must be willing to read and study the scriptures of God.

This sin nature that is on the inside of us has been in us longer than we were aware of the Holy Spirit. Therefore, we should take the opportunity to clean ourselves up by constantly reading and studying the word of truth which are the scriptures of God.

The Holy Spirit is just awaiting the chance to lead us to higher heights in the Lord. We must be willing to submit to the Holy Spirit so that our growth will be maintained. For the spirit is strong, but the flesh is weak, and we can make choices that will make us stumble and fall, but the word of God taught me that He is willing and ready to forgive and pick us up. Ephesians 2:21-22 says, "In whom all the building fitly framed together groweth unto an holy temple in the Lord: In whom ye also are builded together for an habitation of God through the Spirit." The scriptures constantly teach us how to live for God through the Holy Spirit. We must remember that our bodies are the temple of God and in order for Him to abide in us, we must be living by the leadership of the Holy Spirit. In the studying of the holy scriptures, the Holy Spirit will teach us how to grow from level to level, for we know only what we are taught and that it is not about us, but all about Jesus Christ.

In order for the Holy Spirit to dwell within us, we must stay clean and holy. Therefore, repentance and denying of self plays a big part in this walk with the Lord. Our growth depends on how much we submit to the Holy Spirit and obedience to the word of God.

Ephesians 4:14-15 says, "That we henceforth be no more children, tossed to and fro, and carried about with every wind of doctrine, by the sleight of men, and cunning craftiness, whereby they lie in wait to deceive; But speaking the truth in love, may grow up into him in all things, which is the head, even Christ." Paul continuously instructs us that we must not take heed to every teaching that is taught, for we know that there are many who will deceive us. Therefore, it is very important to study the word so that we are not ashamed, rightly dividing the word of truth.

In order for us to grow, we must comprehend the teaching of inspired men and women, as well as study the holy word of God, so that we can be blessed to know the strength and power of God. He said in Romans 8:31, "What shall we then say to these things? If God be for us, who can be against us?" There is much power in those words, for God said that no matter what our enemy tries to do to us, all we have to do is pray to Him and He will tell us how to defeat our enemy. The peace we can receive from the word and from God speaking to us is awesome. Romans 8:33 says, "Who shall lay any thing to the charge of God's elect? It is God that justifieth." Just listen to the master planner give truth, power, strength, healing, joy, peace, and most of all unconditional love. Grace and mercy are with us every day. We just have to give all glory and honor to God.

There is so much more to growing that we can experience when we remember who the creator is and to worship Him in spirit and in truth. There is no way that we can grow without the help of the Lord. For from our mother's womb, we had to depend on our parents for guidance and support. God would also like us to choose Him and the opportunity He has so readily given us to live.

I experienced the awesomeness of God one day in my apartment when the spirit of God came upon me so powerfully that the next thing I knew I was on my knees, and God spoke to me. He said "I give you the air that you breathe, I give you your sight to see," and when He allowed me to get up off my knees, I praised Him for His mercy and grace in allowing me to understand who I was serving. He is a mighty awesome God who deserves all the honor and glory. Thank you God. I love you. Thank you. Give him praise. Hallelujah.

Learn about the word and grow thereby. II Peter 3:18 says, "But grow in grace, and in the knowledge of our Lord and Savior Jesus Christ. To him be glory both now and forever. Amen."

The bottom line... you have to be saved, having accepted Jesus Christ as your Lord and Savior, then living as holy as you can, studying, denying self and growing up in grace. May God bless every reader to understand and gain knowledge and grow up in his darling son, Jesus Christ, through the living Holy Spirit.

GRACE: God's Righteousness At Christ's Expense.

# *Chapter 6*

## Standing

*By whom also we have access by faith into this grace wherein we stand, and rejoice in hope of the glory of God.*

Romans 5:2

In order to be firm and able to stand implies that we have comprehended the laws of the sovereign omnipresent God and have immersed ourselves in the word of God. Therefore, when we gain the ability to speak and do without doubt and fear, then and only then can we convince ourselves that we are serving and living for a holy and righteous God. It takes more than prayer to be able to stand. It will take faith, and not only will we be able to stand, we will be pleasing in God's eyesight. For example let us look at the Hebrew boys, Shadrach, Meshach, and Abednego.

They would not bow to the gods of Nebuchadnezzer and proved that if their God would not deliver them, then they were willing to perish. But their faith kept them safe. Nebuchadnezzar told his men to heat the furnace seven times hotter than usual, and the men did as he commanded them. Then he ordered Shadrach, Meshach, and Abednego to be thrown into the furnace because they refused to bow to a false god. When Nebuchadnezzer's men threw the Hebrew boys into the furnace, his men were killed, but the Hebrew boys were not. When the king looked into the furnace he saw four men not three; he then ordered that the Hebrew boys be brought up out of the fiery furnace. The Hebrew boys had total confidence that God was able to deliver them. Sometimes God uses the word to hit us hard so that we can be jolted into remembering that he, God, is sovereign and will always be there for us, no matter what it looks like. He will never leave us nor forsake us. Remember not to betray him, even as the Hebrew boys did not. Even when they knew that they were being thrown into the furnace, they never doubted God's assurance in deliverance of them.

God knows how much we can stand. Each trial, test, or long-suffering is to strengthen us for the next level in our walk with God through Jesus and the Holy Spirit. Don't defile yourself before God, and don't let the idols of this world deceive you.

Philippians 4:1 says, "Therefore, my brethren dearly beloved and longed for, my joy and crown, so stand fast in the Lord, my dearly beloved." Paul states that God loves us so much that He gave his son for us, so that we could learn how to stand. In order for this to happen, we must be willing to adhere to the work that Jesus has done in order for us to live for eternity. Study the mission and example of Jesus Christ and apply the teachings to your heart. Then and only then will we be able to stand and fight a good fight. Romans 5:1-2 says, "Therefore being justified by faith, we have peace with God through our Lord Jesus Christ: By whom also we have access by faith into this grace wherein we stand, and rejoice in hope of the glory of God." One day I was cooking dinner and thought I had shut the front eye of the stove off, but in reality it was still on. I placed a glass dish on it and was working on the counter beside the stove. As I worked mixing the items to place in the glass bowl, it shattered into many tiny bits of glass. I looked at the situation, saw that the glass had blown past me, gone into the sink, all around me in the area where I was working, onto the pots which were covered, and on the floor all around me was a sea of green glass. Then I looked at myself and noticed that not one tiny bit of glass had touched me. I began to thank God for His mercy and grace for protecting me at that time and moment. Also, I was convinced of serving such a sovereign and wonderful God who cared enough about me that He shielded me from all that glass. Glory hallelujah, hallelujah, hallelujah.

This was one of the many incidents that have occurred in my life that gave me knowledge to be able to stand. The thing that I know is that God loves me and He is no respecter of persons, for what He does for me, He will do for someone else.

The living Holy Spirit is a person who dwells within us and guides us on this glorious walk through Jesus Christ, our Lord and Savior, who wants nothing more than to keep us safe from all hurt, harm and danger and also from ourselves, for sometimes we are our own worst enemy. I Thessalonians 3:8 says, "For now we live, if ye stand fast in the Lord." Jesus would love to be your hiding place from the demons of this wicked world. But, we must submit to God and allow the comforter that Jesus left to lead and guide us through righteousness, so that we can glorify Jesus to His and our Father in heaven. Know that we can stand when we are committed, obedient, holy, serving, faithful, trusting, loving, giving, caring, compassionate, enduring, unselfish, denying self, praying, watching and waiting for our Lord's return, teaching, encouraging, patient, etc., just to name a few virtues to employ when tests, trials and tribulations come and we turn to God and not man, woman or child. God is the only one who can fix any circumstance.

Life is what you make it. God gives us all the resources that are necessary to grow spiritually and prosper and be in good health. It is not easy to stand at times, but when we learn to see the devil and his work for what it is, then we can conquer and gain unbelievable heights in Jesus Christ. Paul said stand when you can't do anything else. Paul was radical for Jesus because he was grateful for Jesus delivering him. He also knew that no matter what the devil threw at him, the power of the living God was able to defeat it and give him the victory. I love Paul's teaching because it has taught me how to stand and be real. I don't have time for foolishness, gossip, hearsay or any other garbage that the devil tries to bring to me. I understand Jesus is the head and not the tail, and I belong to God. Therefore, I submit to God and resist the devil, and he must flee.

Remember God loves us. Therefore, we can stand in faith and be real for our God, for He is sovereign over all. He is the creator, sustainer, and giver of life, our high tower, our salvation, strength, redeemer, protector, fortress and most of all our Daddy.

# *Chapter 7*

## Obtaining

*For whoso findeth me findeth life, and shall obtain
favour of the Lord.*

Proverbs 8:35

Obtaining means to gain success in the daily occupation that
we are striving to achieve in the midst of the hustle and bustle
all around us. In obtaining it is very important how we handle
the issues that arise in our lives. God looks at our motives and
attitude in how we handle issues that arise, and sometimes
what is revealed is not so pretty. Even when our motives are
pure, we have to be able to "maintain in order to obtain" the
desired results. Obtaining comes through experiences and
trials. Many of us don't understand that the circumstances
of life are such that we can be strengthened in this spiritual
walk for a purpose that is given for the pleasure of the Lord
and building up of His kingdom.

Let's look at Jesus, the author and finisher of our lives. Once
He understood the concept for the master plan that God had
for humankind, He didn't hesitate, but pursued the plan with
every ounce of breath and life in Him. Jesus knew that He could
complete every work and purpose God had for Him to accomplish, because His Father and our Father is in total control.

Jesus didn't have to be pumped and primed to know that through the living Holy Spirit, He could be led to victory for the purpose of saving the lives of God's people. Also, Jesus never gave up on the work that was prescribed for Him. He overcame all obstacles that the devil placed in His pathway. Even when the devil tempted Him in the desert, He was on top of the situation. Why? …because He was prayed up. Through prayer, Jesus was strengthened by the angels to continue to go forth. For through it all He understood that He was to glorify God in all that He endured.

This lets us know that in order to gain and maintain the victory, we must suffer and endure hardship. We do know that it is only just a part of the process. This process includes us living a righteous and holy life for the king of kings, lord of lords, so that we may obtain.

Well, in my life I have learned to pray and petition God not only when I am going through hard times, but when things are good in my life, for I know God to be an on-time God. As he told Moses, "I am that I am." I am convinced that should He bring me to it, He will bring me through it. God said to me one day, "There hath no temptation taken you but such as is common to man: but God is faithful, who will not suffer you to be tempted above that ye are able; but will with the temptation also make a way to bear it." When He spoke that into my spirit, I began to cry and praise God for his goodness and mercy upon little old me. It helped me to understand that although God is omnipotent and omnipresent, He still loves a saved sinner like me, who just wants to do His will and know

Him a little better each day. I also understand that this personal relationship with God is not about me, but about how I serve through the Holy Spirit to glorify Jesus to His Father. When I get the pattern right, then I can understand the contract that God provides for us through His divine word. Sometimes God will answer while you are praying; when this happens, I am just overwhelmed by his astounding mercy that I just praise Him at home and wherever I am.

I have learned to praise the One who created me and knew me before I was in my mother's womb and who ordained in me a purposed work before I was born. This just shows me how much God really loves his people and wants to do great and mighty things in their lives.

Saints, I love the Lord because He loved me first, and I can testify that He will answer you. Sometimes you may not like the answer. When this happens, you just thank God and praise Him for his mercy.

Lord, I thank you for teaching me and raising me up to be a vessel, a worker that rightly divides the word of truth so that I am able to obtain the spiritual blessings that You desire for me, and I pray that I am not a stumblingblock for your people.

I understand this life is a personal walk with the Lord in order to let our lights shine for saints and the unsaved, for God's will is that all be saved and not perish. So we must endeavor to do God's will through Jesus and the Holy Spirit in order to help the unsaved have a chance at eternal life. It is our responsibility.

Because someone prayed for us, it is only right that we share the goodness of the Lord with those who do not know Him in the pardon of their sins. For we know that the wages of sin is death and the gift of God is eternal life through Jesus Christ.

The determination of whether we enter heaven is by the choices we make in sharing the word of God spoken into our spirit, accepting Jesus, and being saved. Be encouraged and strengthened in knowing that we serve a God that sits high and looks low, and doesn't mind keeping us, so that we may glorify his son, Jesus Christ, our Lord and Savior.

Obtaining is answered prayer from God, the Father. So watch how you pray, and monitor your motives in asking God for things. He won't grant them if we only want for ourselves or for our personal pleasure. It has to be for a testimony, so that we can glorify Jesus. Remember who and what it is all about: Jesus and salvation for the unsaved. Pray and be blessed. God loves you.

I hope that I have said something that enlightens and strengthens you, my brother or sister. Remember: Jesus is our strength and reason to STAND!!!

# *Summary*
## The Window of Your Understanding

Paul stated in all our getting knowledge, get an understanding. Therefore, we can confidently say that the window of our understanding does not refer to an actual window, but can be compared to one because when we look out a window we can clearly see what is beyond. When we gain knowledge in the word of God, then we can clearly see the justice of the word working to drive and urge us to see more clearly and to walk in confidence, with the majestic God who sits high and looks low. In my gaining understanding, I had to depend totally on God through the Holy Spirit, and the word of God with Jesus at the helm, for the word heals, loves us, guides and justifies us, sanctifies us, teaches us repentance and forgiveness, how to deny ourselves, how to seek Him for compassion and how to treat our brother or sister.

In essence, when we learn to search the scriptures, we learn to submit to God We learn to seek His face on a daily basis, early in the morning, before we do anything else, reading the scriptures every day. Then He teaches us how to obtain favor, stability, build a personal relationship with Him, and wait upon Him. Then we begin to grow, and we can feel a change in our level of growth. Last, but not least, we will be able to stand on the promises of God through Christ Jesus, and lean on the living Holy Spirit and not our own understanding.

Remember we are a peculiar people set apart from the world so that we can glorify Jesus to His Father and our Father. When we are tested, we must understand whether it is of God or the devil. With the strength of the word, we will remain in the steadfastness of the living Holy Spirit who leads us and convicts us when we stray, as when we get an uneasy feeling about what we did or said.

I pray we will be blessed and learn to see out of the window of our understanding with spiritual guidance and love unconditionally for the sake of the gospel.

www.ingramcontent.com/pod-product-compliance
Lightning Source LLC
Chambersburg PA
CBHW021921040426
42448CB00007B/857